I0016369

ARDUINO INTERESTING PROJECTS 3X3X3 LED CUBE, BLUETOOTH CONTROLLED TOY CAR, TONE GENERATOR,MOTOR CONTROL BY FLEX SENSOR ETC..,

CONTENTS

ACKNOWLEDGMENTS

The writer might want to recognize the diligent work of the article group in assembling this book. He might likewise want to recognize the diligent work of the Raspberry Pi Foundation and the Arduino bunch for assembling items and networks that help to make the Internet of Things increasingly open to the overall population. Yahoo for the democratization of innovation!

INTRODUCTION

The Internet of Things (IOT) is a perplexing idea comprised of numerous PCs and numerous correspondence ways. Some IOT gadgets are associated with the Internet and some are most certainly not. Some IOT gadgets structure swarms that convey among themselves. Some are intended for a solitary reason, while some are increasingly universally useful PCs. This book is intended to demonstrate to you the IOT from the back to front. By structure IOT gadgets, the per user will comprehend the essential ideas and will almost certainly develop utilizing the rudiments to make his or her very own IOT applications. These included ventures will tell the per user the best way to assemble their very own IOT ventures and to develop the models appeared. The significance of Computer Security in IOT gadgets is additionally talked about and different systems for protecting the IOT from unapproved clients or programmers. The most significant takeaway from this book is in structure the tasks yourself.

1. DIY 3X3X3 LED CUBE WITH ARDUINO

In this task we are gonna to plan a 3x3x3 LED CUBE as well as associate it to Arduino UNO to get various examples. For a novice we will begin with a basic example.

An ordinary 3*3*3 LED 3D shape associated with UNO is appeared in the picture over, the solid shape comprises of 27 Light Emitting Diodes, these 27 LEDs are organized in lines and segments framing a 3D square.

There are numerous sorts of solid shapes that can be planned. The most straightforward one is 3x3x3 LED shape. For 4*4*4 LED solid shape the work nearly significantly increases since you have to do work for 64 LEDs. With each higher number, the work nearly copies or triples. Be that as it may, each solid shape pretty much takes a shot at a similar way.

3x3x3 LED block is most straightforward in light of the fact that there are certain points of interest to this plan like,

- For this 3D square you need not to stress over power utilization or dispersal.

- Low Power supply request.

- We needn't bother with any exchanging hardware for this block.

- We need lesser rationale terminals so we needn't bother with move registers or anything like that.

We need not stress over power drawn by LED on the grounds that the LED normally expressed to work at 20mA current yet that isn't right, that number gives the greatest current permitted through the LED. Regularly a LED functions admirably from 2mA to 5mA. Anything higher than that, the LED will warm strongly and it will wear out.

So we can drive 9 LEDs conveying 2mA current from a solitary stick of UNO without any issues. The UNO pins are equipped for conveying 20-30mA.

For the 3D shape I picked clear white LED, since I have them save. You can pick any LED sort or shade of your decision, yet the LED with hued will work extraordinary for this undertakings.

For the 3D square we have to save 12 pins of UNO.

Components Required:

ARDUINO UNO, power supply (5v), 220? resisters (3 pieces),

Breadboard wire, 27 white LEDs,

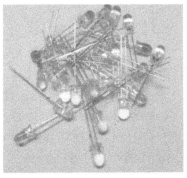 

Soldering wire as well as motion, Welding Iron,

Some instruments, SR2032 button cell,

 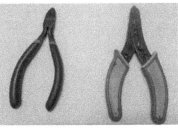

Also, an unfilled cardboard box, pencil, ruler as well as a few jumpers.

Building the Arduino 3x3x3 LED Cube:

Stage 1:

From the start we have to check each LED, when the 3D shape is done if there is any broken LED present in the 3D square it would be hard to supplant, so first we have to check each LED.

This is finished by button cell SR2032, it's a lithium particle battery has a terminal voltage of 3V it is ideal for checking LED, and one can likewise utilize MULTIMETER to check the LED.

In case of affirming all the 27 LEDs are working keep it aside and lets move one to following stage.

Stage 2:

Presently take the breadboard wire and strip the layer off the conveyor, we can utilize any wire however breadboard associating wires works extraordinary. In the wake of stripping off we will have something as appeared in above figure, cut the channel wire in a length of 7cm and proceed with the procedure until we have six 7cm directing wires (figure underneath). These wires are utilized for spanning the LED layers, we will get to this point in the blink of an eye.

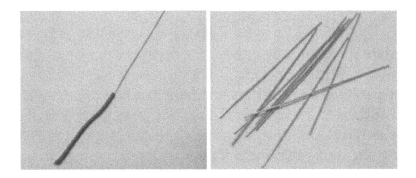

Stage 3:

Presently we have to take the unfilled card board box and stick a white paper on top, as appeared in the figure. The paper is only for denoting the focuses obviously, there is no particular use for it. Simply use cello tape or paste at the corners for holding the paper set up while stamping and penetrating the openings.

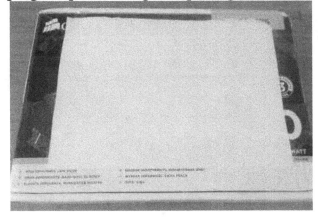

After that take pencil as well as scale, mark nine on paper each 2cm separated framing a structure of 3D shape as appeared in beneath figure.

Here we are utilizing 2cm in light of the fact that; the -ve terminal of LED is of length 2.5cm. So with 2cm separated, we will have 5mm for binding one LED to another. Any length higher from it, the LED terminals patching gets disturbing, with lower length the 3D square looks awkward subsequent to wrapping up. So 2cm would be exceptionally suitable.

After that take a pointy item like a pencil or a pen and jab an opening at each point, ensure you jab a gap pretty much the size of LED, first jab one gap take the LED fit it in, the LED ought not fall through the gap nor the LED ought to the excessively tight. While binding the pins we don't the LED to move so it ought not be lose. On the off chance that the LED is fitted in the gap too tight we can't squirm it out effectively, so each time you jab a gap, check it with the LED.

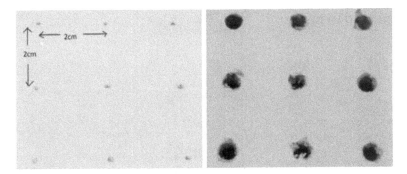

Stage 4:

From that point onward, place a LED in one of the opening and curve the positive terminal as appeared in beneath figure.

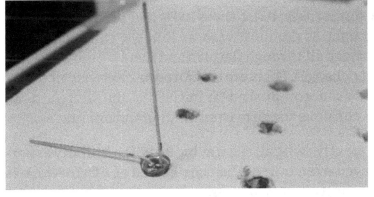

Starting now as well as into the foreseeable future, the positive stick ought to again be twisted to frame a 'L' shape. On close look one can see a little score on the terminal of LED close to the tip, which is the place you should twist for 'L' shape. From that point onward, twist the negative terminal to one side. This is appeared in figure:

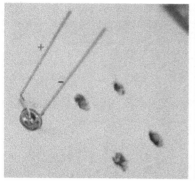 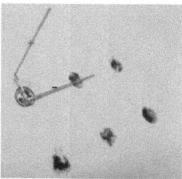

Stage 5:

A similar way twist three LEDs and orchestrate them straight as demonstrated as follows, this example is utilized all through the plan and there would be no further changes. For more comfort one can twist all the 27 LEDs as accomplished for initial one and afterward can be continue to the masterminding and binding.

Presently twist all the staying 24 LEDs similarly as portrayed over, nine of them are bowed as a framework as demonstrated as follows,

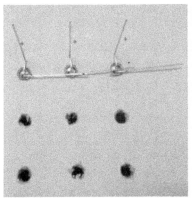 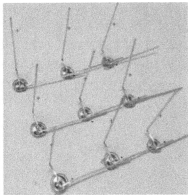

Stage 6:

After that weld all the negative joints, this outcomes in three negative terminals, each speaking to one push. This is demonstrated as follows.

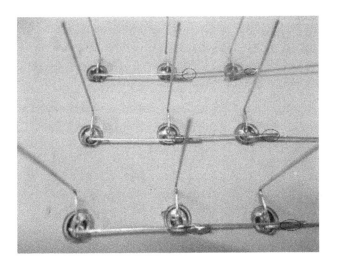

After that take two conveyors wires which we stripped and place them as appeared in the figure and patch the six joints of conduit framing a total grid.

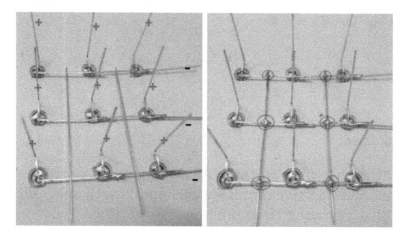

Presently all the negative terminals of nine LEDs are associated with one another with this we will have 9 positive terminals (CP1-CP9) and one negative terminal (CN1). After cautiously squirming out the layer one we will have an arrangement as demonstrated as follows. Cutoff the additional closures and we will have one layer of LED 3D shape.

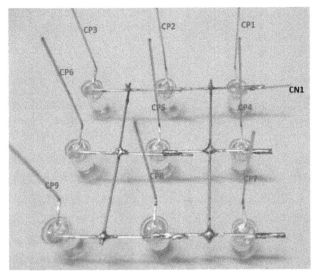

Stage 7:

Presently we have one of three layers of 3D shapes, we have to build up another two layers by following a similar technique as accomplished for this one. Second and third layer are demonstrated as follows:

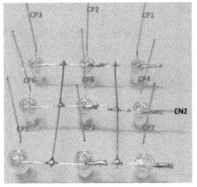
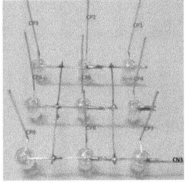

Stage 8:

Presently we have all the three layers expected to make the LED block, we are gonna to stack one over the other to frame a 3D shape.

First we take layer1 and layer 2, mount them one over the other. Bind all the basic positive speaking to terminals. This is appeared in figure. For example CP1 of first layer is patched to CP1 of second layer; CP2 of first layer is welded to CP2 of second layer, etc. Here we will slide the layers about 5mm, one top over the other, first we have to bind the parts of the bargains with the goal that it holds set up and for the layers to be adjusted. Starting now as well as into the foreseeable future, cautiously bind different terminals. Subsequent to patching we will have,

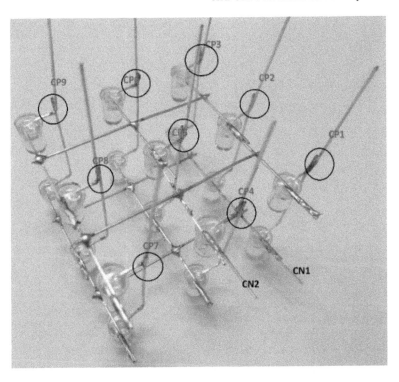

Presently we will stack the third and last layer of 3D shape, with this we have finished the block. The welding of third layer would be somewhat troublesome, as the 3D square terminal be delicate, if the terminals are squirmed excessively, a joint may break inside and fastening an interior joint would be unimaginable, until the 3D square is separate. So one should check each joint twice continuing to the following one.

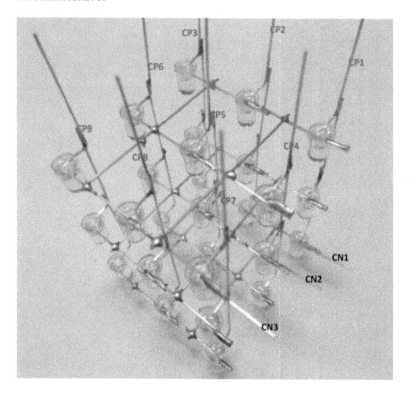

While welding solid shape terminals, the temperature of LED ought to be remembered, if the fastening iron is kept near LED in excess of 5 sec, the LED will burn to the ground and supplanting it would be a torment, so one should focus while patching the LEDs.

Circuit and Working Explanation

With the block total, we have an aggregate of 12 pins. Over which nine are basic positive and three are basic negative. Every basic positive terminal interfaces the positive terminals of three LEDs and every normal negative terminal associates the negative terminals of nine LEDs. So we have nine segments speak to the nine positive terminals (CP1-CP9) and three layers speak to the three negative terminals (CN1-CN3).

PIN2 - - CP1 (Common Positive)

PIN3 - - CP2 (Common Positive)

PIN4 - - CP3 (Common Positive)

PIN5 - - CP4 (Common Positive)

PIN6 - - CP5 (Common Positive)

PIN7 - - CP6 (Common Positive)

PIN8 - - CP7 (Common Positive)

PIN9 - - CP8 (Common Positive)

PIN10 - CP9 (Common Positive)

Stick A0 - - CN1 (Common Negative)

Stick A1 - - CN2 (Common Negative)

Stick A2 - - CN3 (Common Negative)

Presently, we will associate these 12 pins to the UNO properly as appeared in the circuit outline for arduino based LED 3D square beneath.

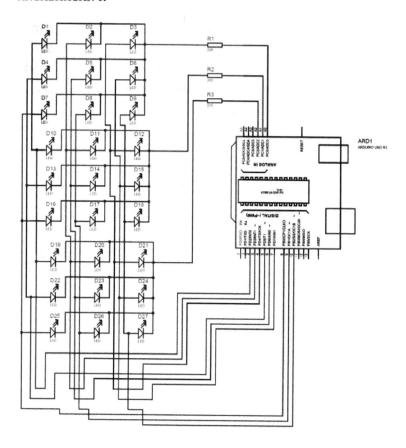

In the event that we need to turn On the single LED for example Driven in the primary layer-second segment, we have to control the CP2 stick and ground the CN1.

With the associations built up, for the LED in the principal layer-second section to sparkle, we have to program the UNO to draw up the PIN3 (which is associated with CP2) and draw down the PIN A0 (associated with CN1).

Every one of the LEDs are associated along these lines, so one can pick which LED to be lit, and the programming for the UNO is done suitably. Here we will give an eternity circle to UNO, to gleam each LED in a steady progression persistently. This cycle continues endlessly until the end of time.

Code

```
void setup()
{
  for (int i=0;i<11;i++)
  {
    pinMode(i,OUTPUT);  // PINS0-10 are set as output
  }
  pinMode(A0,OUTPUT);  //PIN A0 set as output
  pinMode(A1,OUTPUT);  // PIN A1 set as output
  pinMode(A2,OUTPUT);  // PIN A2 set as output


  digitalWrite(A0,HIGH);  //pull up the A0 pin
  digitalWrite(A1,HIGH);  // pull up the A1 pin
  digitalWrite(A2,HIGH);  // pull up the A2 pin
  /* add setup code here, setup code runs once when the processor starts */
}
void loop()
{
      digitalWrite(A0,LOW);    //layer 1 of cube is grounded
```

```
    for (int i=2;i<11;i++)
    {
        digitalWrite(i,HIGH);   //turn ON each LED one
after another in layer1
      delay(200);
       delay(200);
        delay(200);
     digitalWrite(i,LOW);
    }
   digitalWrite(A0,HIGH);  //layer1 is pulled up


        digitalWrite(A1,LOW);   // layer 2 of cube is
grounded
    for (int i=2;i<11;i++)
    {
        digitalWrite(i,HIGH);  // turn ON each LED one
after another in layer2
          delay(200);
          delay(200);
          delay(200);
     digitalWrite(i,LOW);
    }
   digitalWrite(A1,HIGH);  //layer2 is pulled up


        digitalWrite(A2,LOW);     // layer 3 of cube is
grounded
    for (int i=2;i<11;i++)
    {
        digitalWrite(i,HIGH);   // turn ON each LED one
```

after another in layer3

```
        delay(200);
        delay(200);
        delay(200);
    digitalWrite(i,LOW);
    }
    digitalWrite(A2,HIGH);   //layer3 is pulled up
}
```

◆ ◆ ◆

2. IR REMOTE CONTROLLED HOME AUTOMATION UTILIZING ARDUINO

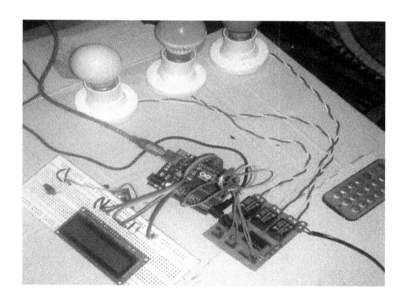

Already we have secured numerous sorts of Home mechanizations utilizing various advancements like DTMF Based Home Automation, PC Controlled Home Automation utilizing Arduino, Bluetooth Controlled Home Automation. In this undertaking, we are using IR based remote correspondence for controlling home apparatuses. In this venture, Arduino is utilized for controlling entire the procedure. We send a few directions to the controlling framework by utilizing IR TV/DVD/MP3 remote for controlling AC home machines. In the wake of accepting sign from IR remote, Arduino sends related sign to transfers which are answerable for turning ON or OFF of the home machines through a hand-off driver.

Working Explanation:

Working of this venture is effectively justifiable. At the point when we press any catch of IR Remote then remote sends a code in type of train of encoded heartbeats utilizing 38Khz regulating recurrence. These heartbeats are gotten by TSOP1738 sensor and read by Arduino and afterward Arduino translates got train of heartbeat into a hex worth and contrasts that decoded worth and the predefined hex estimation of the squeezed catch. In the event that any match happens, at that point Arduino perform relative activity and the comparing result is likewise shown on 16x2 LCD by utilizing suitable directions. Here in this venture we have utilized 3 bulbs of various hues, for exhibition which shows Fan, Light and TV.

There are numerous kinds of IR Remote are accessible for various gadget yet a large portion of them are taken a shot at around 38KHz Frequency signal. Here in this task we control home apparatuses utilizing IR TV remote. For identifying IR remote sign, we use TSOP1738

IR Receiver. This TSOP1738 sensor can detect 38Khz Frequency signal. The working of IR remote as well as the TSOP1738 can be canvassed in detail in this article: IR Transmitter as well as Receiver

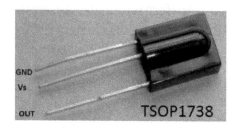

Components:

- Arduino UNO
- IR TV/DVD Remote
- TSOP1738
- Relays 5 volt
- ULN2003
- Connecting wires
- Bulb with holder
- 16x2 LCD
- Bread board
- PVT
- Power supply
- IC 7805

Here in this task we have utilized 7, 8 and 9 number catch of IR remote, for controlling Fan, Light and TV individually and ON/OFF button (Power button) is utilized for killing ON and every apparatuses at the same time.

Here we have utilized switch [EVEN ODD] strategy for ON as well as OFF the single home apparatus. Switch strategy is only to get that whether the catch is squeezed even no of times or the odd no of times. This is found by getting the update in the wake of isolating it by 2 (i%2), on the off chance that there is some update, at that point gadget will be turned ON and in the event that update is 0, at that point it will be killed. Assume Key 7 is pushed on the remote then remote sends a sign to Arduino through TSOP IR Receiver. At that point Arduino translate it and store the decoded an incentive into the outcomes variable. Presently results variable has a hex esteem 0x1FE00FF, subsequent to coordinating it with the predefined hex estimation of key 7 (see above picture), Arduino turns ON the Fan. Presently when we press a similar (key 7) again then IR sends a similar code. Arduino gets same code and coordinated with same code like previously however this time Fan killed in view of flipping the bit [EVEN ODD] (i%2).

Decoding IR Remote Control Signals using Arduino:

Here is a rundown of a DVD NEC type Remote decoded yield codes:

Decimal	Hex	key
33441975	1FE48B7	OFF
33446055	1FE58A7	mode
33454215	1FE7887	mute
33456255	1FE807F	resume
33439935	1FE40BF	previous
33472575	1FEC03F	next
33431775	1FE20DF	EQ
33464415	1FEA05F	volume -
33448095	1FE609F	volume +
33480735	1FEE01F	0
33427695	1FE10EF	RPT
33460335	1FE906F	U/SD
33444015	1FE50AF	1
33478695	1FED827	2
33486855	1FEF807	3
33435855	1FE30CF	4
33468495	1FEB04F	5
33423615	1FE708F	6
33452175	1FE00FF	7
33484815	1FEF00F	8
33462375	1FE9867	9

On the off chance that you don't have the foggiest idea about the Decoded yield for your IR remote, it very well may be effectively discovered, simply pursue these means:

- Download the IR remote library from here https://github.com/z3t0/Arduino-IRremote.

- Unfasten it, and spot it in your Arduino 'Libraries' organizer. At that point rename the extricated envelope to IRremote.

- Run the beneath program from your Arduino and open the Serial Monitor window in Arduino IDE. Presently press any IR Remote catch and see the relating decoded hex yield in Serial Monitor window.

```
* IRremote: IRrecvDemo - demonstrates receiving IR
codes with IRrecv

* An IR detector/demodulator must be connected to
the input RECV_PIN.

* http://arcfn.com

*/

#include <IRremote.h>

int RECV_PIN = 11;

IRrecv irrecv(RECV_PIN);

decode_results results;

void setup()

{
```

```
Serial.begin(9600);

irrecv.enableIRIn(); // Start the receiver

}

void loop() {

if (irrecv.decode(&results)) {

Serial.println(results.value, HEX);

irrecv.resume(); // Receive the next value

}

delay(100);

}
```

The above program is taken from IRremote library's 'models' organizer, you can look at more guides to get familiar with utilizing the IR remote. With the goal that's the means by which we decoded the IR remote yield.

Circuit Description:

Associations of this circuit is basic here a fluid precious stone presentation is utilized for showing status of home machines which is straightforwardly associated with arduino in 4-piece mode. Information pins of LCD to be specific RS, EN, D4, D5, D6, D7 are associated with arduino computerized stick number 6, 7, 8, 9, 10, 11. What's more, yield stick of TSOP1738 is legitimately associated at computerized stick number 14 (An) of Arduino. What's more, Vcc stick is associated a +5 volt and GND stick associated at Ground terminal of circuit. A hand-off driver to be specific ULN2003 is additionally utilized for driving transfers. 5 volt SPDT 3 transfers are utilized for controlling LIGHT, FAN and TV. Furthermore, transfers are associated with arduino stick number 3, 4 and 5 through hand-off driver ULN2003 for controlling LIGHT, FAN and TV individually.

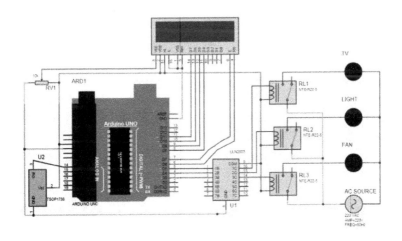

Code Description:

In programming some portion of this venture First of all in programming we incorporates library for IR remote which is effectively accessible at Google. Furthermore, characterize stick and proclaim factors.

```
#include <IRremote.h>

const int RECV_PIN=14;

IRrecv irrecv(RECV_PIN);

decode_results results;
```

And afterward incorporate a header for fluid gem show and afterward we characterizes information as well as control pins for LCD as well as home apparatuses.

```
#include<LiquidCrystal.h>

LiquidCrystal lcd(6,7,8,9,10,11);

#define Fan 3

#define Light 4

#define TV 5
```

After it we have to introduce the LCD and provide guidance of stick that are utilized for fan, light as well as TV.

```
void setup()

{

  Serial.begin(9600);

  lcd.begin(16,2);

  pinMode(Fan, OUTPUT);

  pinMode(Light, OUTPUT);

  pinMode(TV, OUTPUT);
```

As of now clarified, beneath some portion of the code is utilized to contrast the got hex an incentive with effectively characterized hex code of that catch. In the event that it coordinated, at that point a relative activity is performed by utilizing fitting capacities that are given in code.

```
void loop()

{

  if(irrecv.decode(&results))
```

```
{

    Serial.println(results.value,HEX);

    delay(100);

    lcd.setCursor(0,0);

    lcd.print("Fan  Light  TV");

    if(results.value==0x1FE00FF)

    {

      i++;

      int x=i%2;

      digitalWrite(Fan, x);
```

Code

```
#include<LiquidCrystal.h>
#include <IRremote.h>
const int RECV_PIN=14;
IRrecv irrecv(RECV_PIN);
decode_results results;
#include<LiquidCrystal.h>
LiquidCrystal lcd(6,7,8,9,10,11);
#define Fan 3
#define Light 4
```

ARDUINO INTERESTING PROJECTS

```
#define TV 5
int i=0,j=0,k=0,n=0;
void setup()
{
 Serial.begin(9600);
 lcd.begin(16,2);
 pinMode(Fan, OUTPUT);
 pinMode(Light, OUTPUT);
 pinMode(TV, OUTPUT);
 //digitalWrite(13,HIGH);
 lcd.print("Remote Controlled");
 lcd.setCursor(0,1);
 lcd.print("Home Automation");
 delay(2000);
 lcd.clear();
 lcd.print("Hello world");
 lcd.setCursor(0,1);
 delay(1000);
 lcd.print("System Ready...");
 delay(1000);
 irrecv.enableIRIn(); // Start the receiver
 irrecv.blink13(true);
 lcd.clear();
 lcd.setCursor(0,0);
 lcd.print("Fan  Light  TV ");
 lcd.setCursor(0,1);
 lcd.print("OFF  OFF  OFF");
}
void loop()
{
```

ANBAZHAGAN K

```
if(irrecv.decode(&results))
{
 Serial.println(results.value,HEX);
 delay(100);
 lcd.setCursor(0,0);
 lcd.print("Fan Light TV");
 if(results.value==0x1FE00FF)
 {
  i++;
  int x=i%2;
  digitalWrite(Fan, x);
  lcd.setCursor(0,1);
  if(x)
  lcd.print("ON ");
  else
  lcd.print("OFF ");
  // delay(200);
 }


  else if(results.value==0x1FEF00F)  // key 1
 {
  j++;
  int x=j%2;
  digitalWrite(Light, x);
  lcd.setCursor(6,1);
  if(x)
  lcd.print("ON ");
  else
  lcd.print("OFF ");
  // delay(200);
```

```
}


  if(results.value==0x1FE9867)
{
 k++;
 int x=k%2;
 digitalWrite(TV, x);
 lcd.setCursor(13,1);
 if(x)
 lcd.print("ON ");
 else
 lcd.print("OFF");
 // delay(200);
 }



    if(results.value==0x1FE48B7)
{
 n++;
 int x=n%2;
 digitalWrite(TV, x);
 digitalWrite(Fan,x);
 digitalWrite(Light,x);
 lcd.setCursor(0,1);
 if(x)
 lcd.print("ON  ON  ON ");
 else
 lcd.print("OFF  OFF  OFF");
 //delay(200);
 }
```

```
  irrecv.resume(); // Receive the next value
  //delay(100);
 }
}
```

◆ ◆ ◆

3. BLUETOOTH CONTROLLED TOY CAR UTILIZING ARDUINO

In the wake of creating hardly any prevalent auto-mated ventures like line devotee robot, edge maintain-ing a strategic distance from robot, DTMF robot, signal controlled robot, and so on in this undertaking we will build up a bluetooth controlled robo vehicle. Here we utilized a Bluetooth module to control the vehicle, and it is additionally an android based application.

Components

- Arduino UNO
- Bluetooth module HC-05
- DC Motors
- 9 Volt Battery as well as 6 volt battery
- Motor Driver L293D
- Toy Car
- Battery Connector

Bluetooth controlled vehicle is constrained by utilizing Android cell phone rather than some other strategy like catches, signal and so forth. Here just needs to contact button in android telephone to control the vehicle in forward, backwardd, left and right bearings. So here android telephone is utilized as transmitting gadget and Bluetooth module put in vehicle is utilized as recipient. Android telephone will transmit order utilizing its in-assembled Bluetooth to vehicle with the goal that it can move in the necessary course like pushing ahead, switch, turning left, turning right and stop.

Bluetooth Module

HC Bluetooth module comprises two things one is Bluetooth sequential interface module and a Bluetooth connector. Bluetooth sequential module is utilized for changing over sequential port to Bluetooth.

How to work Bluetooth module?

You can straightforwardly utilize the Bluetooth module as a result of buying from showcase, considering the way that there is no compelling reason to change any setting of bluetooth module. Default baud pace of new Bluetooth module is 9600 bps. You simply need to associate rx and tx to controller or sequential converter and give 5 volt dc managed power supply to module.

Bluetooth module has two modes one is ace mode and second one is slave mode. Client can set either mode by utilizing some AT directions. Indeed, even client can set module's setting by utilizing AT direction. Here is a few directions uses are given:

Most importantly client need to enter AT mode with 38400 bps baud rate by squeezing EN button at Bluetooth module or by giving HIGH level at EN stick. Note: all directions should closes with \r\n (0x0d and 0x0a) or ENTER KEY from console.

After it in the event that you send AT to module, at that point module will react with OK

AT ? Test Command

AT+ROLE=0 ? Slave Mode select

AT+ROLE=1 ? Master Mode select

AT+NAME=xyz ? Set Bluetooth Name

AT+PSWD=xyz ? Set Password

AT+UART=<value1>,<value2>,<value3> ? set Baud

rate

Eg. AT+UART=9600,0,0

Stick Description of accelerometer

- STATE ? Open

- Rx ? Serial getting pin

- Tx ? Serial transmitting pin

- GND ? ground

- Vcc ? +5volt dc

- EN ? to enter in AT mode

Working Explanation

In this venture we have utilized a toy vehicle for exhibit. Here we have chosen a RF toy vehicle with moving left right controlling element. In the wake of purchasing this vehicle we have supplanted its RF circuit with our Arduino circuit. This vehicle have two dc engines at its front and back side. Front side engine is utilized for provide guidance to vehicle means turning left or right side (like genuine vehicle directing component). What's more, back side engine is utilized for driving the vehicle in forward and in reverse heading. A Bluetooth module is utilized to get direction from android telephone and Arduino UNO is utilized for controlling the entire framework.

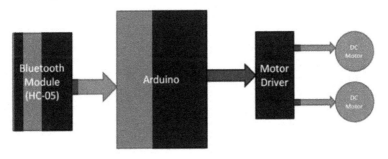

Bluetooth controlled vehicle moves as indicated by catch contacted in the android Bluetooth portable application. To run this task first we have to download Bluetooth application structure Google play store. We can utilize any Bluetooth application that supporting or can send information. Here are some applications' name that may work accurately.

- Bluetooth Spp professional

- Bluetooth controller

In the wake of introducing application you have to open it and afterward search Bluetooth gadget and select wanted Bluetooth gadget. And afterward arrange keys. Here in this undertaking we have utilized Bluetooth controller application.

- Download and introduce Bluetooth Controller.

- Turned ON portable Bluetooth.

- Presently open Bluetooth controller application

- Press filter

- Select wanted Bluetooth gadget

- Presently set keys by squeezing set fastens on screen. To set keys we have to squeeze 'set catch' and set key as indicated by picture given beneath:

In the wake of setting keys press alright.

At the point when we contact forward catch in Blue-tooth controller application then vehicle start moving forward way and pushing proceeds ahead until next direction comes.

At the point when we contact in reverse catch in Blue-tooth controller application then vehicle start moving backward heading and moving proceeds with turn around until next direction comes.

At the point when we contact left catch in Bluetooth controller application then vehicle start moving left way and moving proceeds with left until next order comes. In this condition front side engine turns front side wheels left way and back engine runs forward way.

At the point when we contact right catch in Bluetooth controller application then vehicle start moving right way and moving proceeds with directly until next order comes. In this condition front side engine turns front side wheels right way and back engine runs forward way.

Furthermore, by contacting stop button we can stop the vehicle.

Circuit Diagram and Explanation

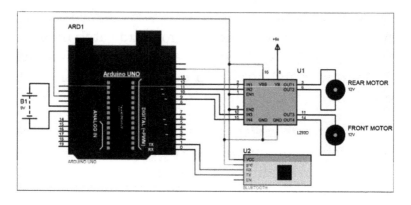

Circuit outline for bluetooth controlled vehicle is appeared in above figure. A Motor driver is associated with arduino to run the vehicle. Engine driver's information pins 2, 7, 10 and 15 are associated with arduino's computerized stick number 12, 11, 10 and 9 individually. Here we have utilized two DC engines to driver vehicle in which one engine is associated at yield stick of engine driver 3 and 6 and another engine is associated at 11 and 14. A 6 volt Battery is likewise used to control the engine driver for driving engines. Bluetooth module's rx as well as tx pins are straightforwardly associated at tx as well as rx of Arduino. Furthermore, vcc and ground stick of Bluetooth module is associated at +5 volt and gnd of Arduino. What's more, a 9 volt battery is utilized for control the circuit at Arduino's Vin stick

Program Explanation

In program above all else we have characterized yield

pins for engines.

```
#define m11 11   // rear motor

#define m12 12

#define m21 10   // front motor

#define m22 9
```

And afterward in arrangement, we offered bearings to stick.

```
void setup()

{

  Serial.begin(9600);

  pinMode(m11, OUTPUT);

  pinMode(m12, OUTPUT);

  pinMode(m21, OUTPUT);

  pinMode(m22, OUTPUT);

}
```

After this we read contribution by utilizing sequential correspondence structure Bluetooth module and play out the activity as needs be.

```
void loop()

{

  while(Serial.available())

  {

    char ch=Serial.read();

    str[i++]=ch;

    if(str[i-1]=='1')

    {

    Serial.println("Forward");

    forward();

    i=0;

    }

    else if(str[i-1]=='2')
```

```
{

  Serial.println("Left");

  right();

  i=0;

}

else if(str[i-1]=='3')

{

  Serial.println("Right");

  left();

  i=0;

}
```

At that point we have made capacities for various headings of vehicle. There are five conditions for this Bluetooth controlled vehicle which are utilized to give the bearings:

Touched button in Bluetooth controller app	Output for front side motor to give direction	Output for rear side motor to move forward or reverse direction	

Button	M11	M12	M21	M22	Direction
Stop	0	0	0	0	Stop
Forward	0	0	0	1	Forward
Backward	0	0	1	0	Backward
Right	1	0	0	1	Right
left	0	1	0	1	Left

Code

```
#define m11 11   // rear motor
#define m12 12
#define m21 10   // front motor
#define m22 9
char str[2],i;
void forward()
{
  digitalWrite(m11, LOW);
  digitalWrite(m12, LOW);
  digitalWrite(m21, HIGH);
  digitalWrite(m22, LOW);
}
void backward()
{
  digitalWrite(m11, LOW);
  digitalWrite(m12, LOW);
  digitalWrite(m21, LOW);
  digitalWrite(m22, HIGH);
}
void left()
{
```

```
digitalWrite(m11, HIGH);
digitalWrite(m12, LOW);
delay(100);
digitalWrite(m21, HIGH);
digitalWrite(m22, LOW);
}
void right()
{
digitalWrite(m11, LOW);
digitalWrite(m12, HIGH);
delay(100);
digitalWrite(m21, HIGH);
digitalWrite(m22, LOW);
}
void Stop()
{
digitalWrite(m11, LOW);
digitalWrite(m12, LOW);
digitalWrite(m21, LOW);
digitalWrite(m22, LOW);
}
void setup()
{
Serial.begin(9600);
pinMode(m11, OUTPUT);
pinMode(m12, OUTPUT);
pinMode(m21, OUTPUT);
pinMode(m22, OUTPUT);
}
void loop()
```

```
{
 while(Serial.available())
 {
  char ch=Serial.read();
  str[i++]=ch;


   if(str[i-1]=='1')
  {
  Serial.println("Forward");
  forward();
  i=0;
  }
  else if(str[i-1]=='2')
  {
  Serial.println("Left");
  right();
  i=0;
  }
  else if(str[i-1]=='3')
  {
   Serial.println("Right");
   left();
   i=0;
  }


   else if(str[i-1]=='4')
  {
   Serial.println("Backward");
   backward();
```

```
  i=0;
 }
 else if(str[i-1]=='5')
 {
  Serial.println("Stop");
  Stop();
  i=0;
 }
 delay(100);
 }
}
```

❖ ❖ ❖

4. SERVO POSITION CONTROL WITH WEIGHT (FORCE SENSOR)

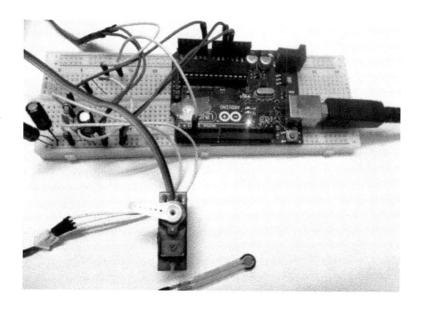

In this instructional exercise we will build up a circuit utilizing Force sensor, Arduino Uno as well as a servo engine. It will be a servo control framework where the servo shaft position is controlled by the weight present on the power sensor. Before going any additionally how about we talk about the servo and different segments.

Servo Motors are utilized where there is a requirement for precise shaft development or position. These are not proposed for fast applications. These are proposed for low speed, medium torque as well as precise position application. These engines are utilized in mechanical arm machines, flight controls and control frameworks. Servo engines are likewise utilized in some of printers and fax machines.

Servo engines are accessible at various shapes as well as sizes. A servo engine will have generally there wires, one is for positive voltage another is for ground and last one is for position setting. The RED wire is associated with control, Black wire is associated with ground and YELLOW wire is associated with signal.

A servo engine is a blend of DC engine, position control framework, gears. The situation of the pole of the DC engine is balanced by the control gadgets in the servo, in light of the obligation proportion of the PWM signal the SIGNAL stick. Basically the control hardware modify shaft position by controlling DC engine. This information in regards to position of shaft is sent through the SIGNAL stick. The position information to the control ought to be sent as PWM signal through the Signal stick of servo engine.

The recurrence of PWM (Pulse Width Modulated) sign can change dependent on kind of servo engine. The significant thing here is the DUTY RATIO of the PWM signal. In view of this DUTY RATION the control hardware change the pole.

As appeared in beneath figure, for the pole to be moved to 9o clock the TURN ON RATION must be 1/18.ie. 1milli second of 'ON schedule' as well as 17milli second of 'OFF time' in a 18ms sign.

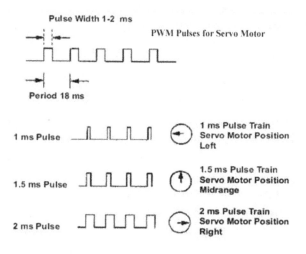

For the pole to be moved to 12o clock the ON time of sign must be 1.5ms and OFF time ought to be 16.5ms.

This proportion is decoded by control framework in servo and it alters the position dependent on it.

This PWM in here is produced by utilizing ARDUINO UNO.

So for the time being we realize that, we can control the

SERVO MOTOR shaft by fluctuating the obligation proportion of PWM sign created by UNO.

Presently how about we talk about power sensor or weight sensor.

To interface a FORCE sensor with ARDUINO UNO, we are gonna utilize 8 piece ADC highlight in arduno uno.

A FORCE sensor is a transducer which changes its opposition when weight is applied on surface. Power sensor is accessible in various sizes and shapes.

We are gonna to utilize one of the less expensive adaptations since we needn't bother with quite a bit of precision here. FSR400 is the most affordable power sensors in the market. The image of FSR400 is appeared in underneath figure.

Presently note that the FSR 400 is touchy along the length, the power or weight ought to be focused on the labyrinth on the center of eye of sensor, as appeared in figure.

In the event that the power is applied at wrong occasions the gadget could harm forever.

Another significant thing to realize that, the sensor can drive flows of high go. So remember the driving flows while introducing. Additionally the sensor has a point of confinement on power that is 10Newtons. So we can apply just 1Kg of weight. In the event that loads higher than 1Kg applied the sensor may give a few deviations.

In the event that it's expanded more than 3Kg. the sensor may harm for all time.

As advised before this sensor is utilized to detect the adjustments in pressure. So when the weight is applied over FORCE sensor, the obstruction is changed radically. The opposition of FS400 over weight is appeared in underneath diagram:

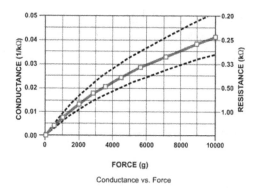

Conductance vs. Force

As shown in above figure, the opposition among the 2 contacts of sensor diminishes with weight or the conductance among 2 contacts of sensor increments.

The opposition of an unadulterated conductor is given by:

$$R = \frac{\rho l}{A}$$

Where,

p-Resistivity of conductor

l= Length of conductor

A= Area of conductor.

Presently consider a conductor with opposition "R", if some weight is applied over conductor, the zone on conductor diminishes and the length of conductor increments because of weight. So by equation the opposition of conductor should increment, as the obstruction R is conversely relative to territory and furthermore straightforwardly corresponding to length l.

So with this for a conductor under strain or weight the opposition of conductor increments. Be that as it may, this change is little contrasted with generally opposition. For an extensive change numerous conductors are stacked together.

This is the thing that occurs inside the Power Sensors appeared in above figure. On looking carefully one can sees numerous lines inside the sensor. Every one of these lines speaks to a conductor. Affectability of sensor is in conductor numbers.

Be that as it may, for this situation the opposition will diminish with pressure in light of the fact that the material utilized here is definitely not an unadulterated conductor. The FSR here are strong polymer thick film gadgets. So these are not unadulterated conductor material gadgets. These are comprised of a material, that display a reduction in opposition with increment in power applied to the outside of the sensor.

This material shows qualities as appeared in chart of FSR.

This adjustment in obstruction can do nothing more than trouble except if we can understand them. The current controller can just peruse the odds in voltage and nothing less, for this we are going to utilize voltage divider circuit, with that we can determine the opposition change as voltage change.

Voltage divider is a resistive circuit and is appeared in figure. In this resistive system we have one consistent opposition and other variable obstruction. As appeared in figure, R1 here is a consistent opposition and R2 is FORCE sensor which goes about as an obstruction.

The midpoint of branch is taken to estimation. With R2 change, we have change at Vout. So with this we have a voltage which changes with weight.

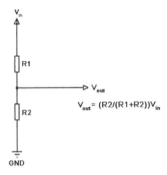

$$V_{out} = (R2/(R1+R2))V_{in}$$

Presently significant thing to note here is, the information taken by the controller for ADC transformation is as low as 50μAmp. This stacking impact of obstruction based voltage divider is significant as the current drawn from Vout of voltage divider expands the mistake rate increments, until further notice we need not stress over stacking impact.

Presently when the power is applied on the FORCE SENSOR, the voltage at divider end changes this stick as associated with ADC channel of UNO, we will get an alternate advanced an incentive from ADC of UNO, at whatever point power on sensor changes.

This ADC advanced worth is coordinated to the obligation proportion of PWM signal, so we have the SERVO position control in connection to power applied on sensor.

Components

Equipment: UNO, control supply (5v), 1000uF capacitor, 100nF capacitor (Three pieces), 100K? resistor, SERVO MOTOR (SG 90), 220? resistor, FSR400 power sensor.

Programming: Atmel studio 6.2 or aurdino daily.

Circuit Diagram and Working Explanation

The circuit outline for servo engine control by power sensor is appeared in underneath figure.

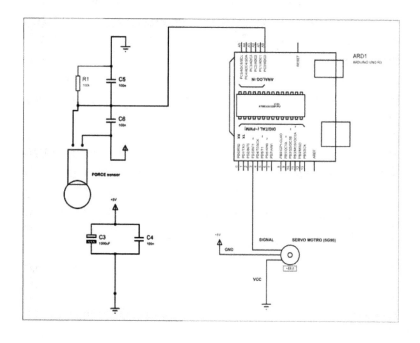

The voltage crosswise over sensor isn't totally straight; it will be an uproarious one. To sift over the commotion a capacitors are put over every resistor in the divider circuit as appeared in figure.

Here we are going to take the voltage gave by the divider (voltage which speaks to weight straightly) and feed it into one of ADC channels of Arduino Uno. After change we are gonna to take that advanced worth (speaking to weight) and relate it to PWM esteem and give this PWM sign to SERVO engine.

So with weight we have a PWM esteem which changes its obligation proportion contingent upon advanced worth. Higher the computerized worth higher the obligation proportion of PWM. So with higher obligation proportion PWM signal, the servo shaft should arrive at the extreme right or far left according to the figure gave in the presentation.

On the off chance that the weight is lower, we will have lower PWM obligation proportion and according to the figure in presentation the servo should the arrive at the extreme right.

With this we have a SERVO position manage by WEIGHT or FORCE.

For this to happened we have to set up scarcely any guidelines in program and we will discuss them in detail beneath.

ARDUINO has six ADC channels, as show in figure. In those any one or every one of them can be utilized as contributions for simple voltage. The UNO ADC is of

10 piece goals (so the number qualities from (0-(2^10) 1023)).This implies that it will guide input voltages somewhere in the range of 0 and 5 volts into whole number qualities somewhere in the range of 0 and 1023. So for each (5/1024= 4.9mV) / unit.

Here we are gonna to utilize A0 of UNO. We have to know a couple of things.

1. analogRead(pin);
2. analogReference();
3. analogReadResolution(bits);

As a matter of first importance the Arduino Uno ADC channels has a default reference estimation of 5V. This implies we can give a greatest information voltage of 5V for ADC transformation at any info channel. Since certain sensors give voltages from 0-2.5V, with a 5V reference we get lesser precision, so we have a guidance that empowers us to change this reference esteem. So for changing the reference esteem we have ("analogReference();") For now we leave it as.

As default we get the most extreme board ADC goals which is 10bits, this goals can be changed by utilizing guidance ("analogReadResolution(bits);"). This goals change can prove to be useful for certain cases. Until further notice we leave it as.

Presently if the above conditions are set to default,

the we can peruse an incentive from ADC of channel '0' by legitimately calling capacity "analogRead(pin);", here "stick" speaks to stick where we associated simple sign, for this situation it would be "A0". The incentive from ADC can be taken into a whole number as "int SEN-SORVALUE = analogRead(A0); ", by this guidance the incentive after ADC gets put away in the number "SEN-SORVALUE".

The PWM of UNO can accomplished at any of pins symbolized as " ~ " on the PCB board. There are six PWM directs in UNO. We are gonna to utilize PIN3 for our motivation.

analogWrite(3,VALUE);

From above condition we can straightforwardly get the PWM signal at the relating pin. The first parameter in quite a while is for picking the stick number of PWM signal. Second parameter is for composing obligation proportion.

The PWM estimation of Arduino Uno can be changed since 0 to 255. With "0" as most minimal to "255" as most elevated. With 255 as obligation proportion we will get 5V at PIN3. On the off chance that the obligation proportion is given as 125 we will get 2.5V at PIN3.

Presently we should discuss the servo engine control, the Arduino Uno has a component which empowers us to control the servo situation by simply giving the degree esteem. State in case we need the servo to be at 30, we can legitimately speak to the incentive in the program. The SERVO header document deals with all the obligation proportion counts inside. You can get familiar with servo engine control with arduino here.

Presently the sg90 can move from 0-180 degrees, we have ADC result 0-1024.

So ADC is around multiple times the SERVO POSITION. So by isolated the ADC result by 6 we will get the inexact SERVO hand position. Subsequently we have a PWM signal whose obligation proportion changes directly with WEIGHT or FORCE. This being given to servo engine, we can manage the servo engine by power sensor.

Code

```
#include <Servo.h> //header for controller servo
Servo servo; //keeping name of servo SERVO itself
int sensorvalue =0;
void setup()
{
    pinMode(A0,INPUT); //force sensor value input
    pinMode(3,OUTPUT); //PWM output to servo
    servo.attach(3); //telling where signal pin of servo
attached(must be a PWM pin)
}
void loop()
```

```
{
    sensorvalue = analogRead(A0); //read analog value from sensor
    servo.write(sensorvalue/6); //set servo position based on ADC result
}
```

❖ ❖ ❖

5. HOW TO SET UP UART CORRESPONDENCE AMONG ATMEGA8 AND ARDUINO UNO?

Here we will build up a correspondence among an ATmega8 microcontroller as well as Arduino Uno. The correspondence set up here is UART (Universal Asynchronous Receiver Transmitter) type. It's sequential correspondence. By this sequential correspondence information can be shared between two controllers, which is a required in different implanted framework applications.

In inserted frameworks we should have essential learning about framework interchanges, so for this we are doing this venture. In this venture we will talk about fundamental correspondence framework and we will send a few information from transmitter to recipient in sequential.

[Also check: UART correspondence between two ATmega controllers]

In this task ATMEGA8 goes about as a TRANSMITTER and ARDUINO UNO goes about as a RECECIVER. In sequential correspondence we will send information BIT BY BIT, until a BYTE of information is moved totally. The information can be of 10bit size yet we will keep to 8BITS until further notice.

Components Required

Equipment: ATMEGA8, ARDUINO UNO, control supply (5v), AVR-ISP PROGRAMMER, 100uF capacitor (associated crosswise over power supply), 1K? resistor (two pieces), LED, Button.

Programming: Atmel studio 6.1, progisp or streak enchantment, ARDUINO NIGHTLY.

Circuit Diagram and Explanation

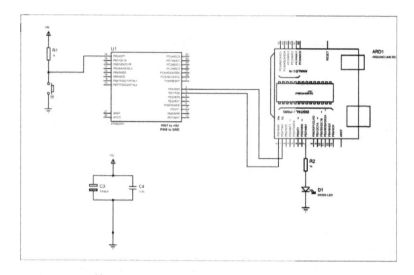

Before we talk about the circuit outline and programming for transmitter and collector, we have to comprehend about the sequential correspondence. The ATMEGA here sends information to the UNO in sequential as talked about before.

It has different methods of correspondence like MASTER SLAVE correspondence, JTAG correspondence however for simple correspondence we are picking RS232. Here we will associate the TXD (Transmitter) PIN of ATMEGA8 to RXD (Receiver) PIN of ARDUINO UNO

The information correspondence set up is customized to have:

- Eight information bits

- Two stop bits

- No equality check bit

- Baud pace of 9600 BPS(Bits Per Second)

- Offbeat communication(No clock share among ATMEGA8 and UNO (both have diverse clock units))

For building up UART between Arduino Uno and ATMEGA8 we have to program the setting precisely. For this we have to keep the previously mentioned parameters same at the two finishes. In this one goes about as TRANSMITTER and different goes about as RECEIVER. We will examine each side settings beneath.

Presently for the RS232 interface, the accompanying highlights must be fulfilled for the TRANSMITTER side (ATMEGA8):

1. The TXD stick (information accepting component) of first controller must be empowered for TRANSMITTER.

2. Since the correspondence is sequential we have to know at whatever point the information bye is gotten, with the goal that we can stop the program until complete byte is gotten. This is finished by empowering an information get total intrude.

3. Information is transmitted and got to controller in

8bit mode. So two characters will be sent to the controller at once.

4. There are no equality bits, one stop bit in the information sent by the module.

The above highlights are set in the controller registers; we will talk about them quickly:

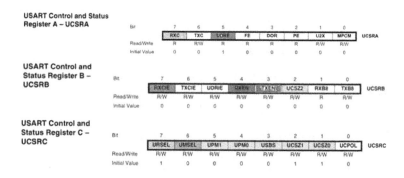

Dull Gray (UDRE): This bit not set during startup however it is utilized during attempting to check whether transmitter is prepared to transmit or not. See the program on TRASMITTER SIDE for more subtleties.

VOILET (TXEN): This bit is set for empowering transmitter stick on TRASMITTER SIDE.

YELLOW (UCSZ0, UCSZ1, and UCSZ2): These three bits are utilized for choosing the quantity of information bits we are getting or sending in a solitary go.

UCSZ Bits Settings

UCSZ2	UCSZ1	UCSZ0	Character Size
0	0	0	5-bit
0	0	1	6-bit
0	1	0	7-bit
0	1	1	8-bit
1	0	0	Reserved
1	0	1	Reserved
1	1	0	Reserved
1	1	1	9-bit

The correspondence between different sides is set up as eight piece correspondence. By coordinating the correspondence with table we have, UCSZ0, UCSZ1 to one and UCSZ2 to zero.

ORANGE (UMSEL): This bit is set dependent on whether the framework is conveying nonconcurrently (both use distinctive clock) or synchronously (both use same clock).

UMSEL Bit Settings

UMSEL	Mode
0	Asynchronous Operation
1	Synchronous Operation

Both the SYTEMS don't share any clock. Since them two utilize interior clock of their own. So we have to set UMSEL to 0 in the two controllers.

GREEN (UPM1, UPM0): These two bits are balanced dependent on bit equality we are utilizing in correspondence.

UPM Bits Settings

UPM1	UPM0	Parity Mode
0	0	Disabled
0	1	Reserved
1	0	Enabled, Even Parity
1	1	Enabled, Odd Parity

The information ATMEGA here is customized to send information with no equality, as the information transmission length is little, we can plainly anticipate no information misfortune or mistake. So we are not setting any equality here. So we set both UPM1, UPM0 to zero or they are left, since all bits are 0 of course.

BLUE (USBS): This bit is utilized for picking the quantity of stop bits we are utilizing during correspondence.

USBS Bit Settings

USBS	Stop Bit(s)
0	1-bit
1	2-bit

The correspondence set up her is of offbeat kind, so for getting progressively precise information transmission and gathering, we have to utilize two stop bits, Hence we set USBS to '1' in TRANSMITTER side..

The baud rate is set in controller by picking the fitting UBRRH:

USART Baud Rate Registers – UBRRL and UBRRH

Bit	15	14	13	12	11	10	9	8	
	URSEL	–	–	–		UBRR[11:8]			UBRRH
	UBRR[7:0]								UBRRL
	7	6	5	4	3	2	1	0	
Read/Write	R/W	R	R	R	R/W	R/W	R/W	R/W	
	R/W	R/W	R/W	R/W	R/W	R/W	R/W	R/W	
Initial Value	0	0	0	0	0	0	0	0	
	0	0	0	0	0	0	0	0	

The UBRRH worth is picked by cross alluding baud rate and CPU precious stone recurrence:

Examples of UBRR Settings for Commonly Used Oscillator Frequencies

Baud Rate (bps)	f_{osc} = 1.0000 MHz				f_{osc} = 1.8432 MHz				f_{osc} = 2.0000 MHz			
	U2X = 0		U2X = 1		U2X = 0		U2X = 1		U2X = 0		U2X = 1	
	UBRR	Error	UBRR	Error	UBRR	Error	UBRR	Error	UBRR	Error	UBRR	Error
2400	25	0.2%	51	0.2%	47	0.0%	95	0.0%	51	0.2%	103	0.2%
4800	12	0.2%	25	0.2%	23	0.0%	47	0.0%	25	0.2%	51	0.2%
9600	6	-7.0%	12	0.2%	11	0.0%	23	0.0%	12	0.2%	25	0.2%
14.4k	3	8.5%	8	-3.5%	7	0.0%	15	0.0%	8	-3.5%	16	2.1%
19.2k	2	8.5%	6	-7.0%	5	0.0%	11	0.0%	6	-7.0%	12	0.2%

So by cross reference UBRR worth is viewed as '6', thus the baud rate is set.

With this we have built up settings on TRANSMITTER SIDE; we will discuss RECEIVING SIDE at this point.

The sequential correspondence empowering in UNO should be possible by utilizing a solitary order.

1. Serial.begin(9600);
2. receiveddata = Serial.read();

The correspondence we dared to build up is finished by a BAUD pace of 9600 bits for each second. So for UNO to set up such baud rate and to begin sequential correspondence we use direction "Serial.begin(9600);". Here 9600 is baud rate and is variable.

Presently all left if to get information, one an information is gotten by the UNO, it will be accessible for taking. This information is gotten by direction "receiveddata = Serial.read();". By this order sequential information is taken to 'receiveddata' named whole number.

As appeared in circuit a catch in associated on transmitter side, when this catch in squeezed an eight piece information is sent by TRANSMITTER (ATMEGA8) and this information is gotten by RECEIVER (ARDUINO UNO). On accepting this information effectively it flips the LED combined with it ON and OFF, to show fruitful information move between two controller.

By this UART correspondence between ATMEGA8 controller and ARDUINO UNO is effectively settled.

Code

PROGRAM ON TRANSMITTER SIDE:

```
#include <avr/io.h>
//header to enable data flow control over pins
#define F_CPU 1000000UL
//telling controller crystal frequency attached
#include <util/delay.h>
//header to enable delay function in program
int main(void)
{
```

```
DDRB =0;//PORTB is set as INPUT
DDRD |= 1 << PIND1;//pin1 of portD as OUTPUT
DDRD &= ~(1 << PIND0);//pin0 of portD as INPUT
PORTD |= 1 << PIND0;
    int UBBRValue = 6;//AS described before setting baud rate 9600BPS
//Put the upper part of the baud number here (bits 8 to 11)
UBRRH = (unsigned char) (UBBRValue >> 8);
//Put the remaining part of the baud number here
UBRRL = (unsigned char) UBBRValue;
//Enable the receiver and transmitter
UCSRB = (1 << RXEN) | (1 << TXEN);
//Set 2 stop bits and data bit length is 8-bit
UCSRC = (1 << USBS) | (3 << UCSZ0);
while (1)
{
        if (bit_is_clear(PINC,0))//once button is pressed
        {
            while (! (UCSRA & (1 << UDRE)) );
            {
                UDR = 0b11110000;//once transmitter is ready sent eight bit data
            }
            _delay_ms(220);
        }
```

PROGRAM ON RECEIVER SIDE:

```
int receiveddata =0;
void setup()
{
        Serial.begin(9600);//serial data rate is set for
9600BPS
    pinMode(0,INPUT);//RXD pin is set for INPUT
    pinMode(1,OUTPUT);
        pinMode(7,OUTPUT);//PIN1,PIN7 are set for
output
}
void loop()
{
        if (Serial.available() > 0) //if data received is
available
        {
    receiveddata = Serial.read();//read serial data avail-
able
            if (receiveddata == 0)//compare the data
received
            {
                PORTD^=(1<<7);//id data matches
toggle the LED.
            }
        }
}
```

6. ARDUINO BASED TONE GENERATOR

In this venture we will build up a tone generator utilizing Arduino Uno. We will have catches interfaced with the UNO as well as each and every one of them creates diverse power of tone. The recurrence of tone created by the UNO is same at each inside. It's the power of the sound which changes with each press. This is the one of the least demanding approach to make a piano with Arduino Uno. Likewise check this Piano circuit.

The tones can be expanded up to 20. This gives the best tone variety and much smoother changes. The force of the tone is changed by Pulse Width Modulation. A case of PWM is appeared in beneath diagram.

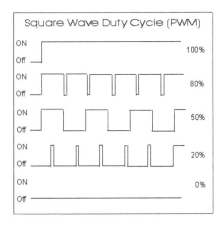

In PWM, the recurrence of sign or the timeframe of sign (Ton + Toff) is constantly consistent. Just the proportion of TURN ON as well as TURN OFF time changes. For instance in the second diagram in above figure, the TURN ON time is 80% and TURN OFF time is 20% of complete term.

In the third diagram, the TURN ON time is half as well as TURN OFF time is half of complete length. So in first case we have a commitment proportion of 80% and in second case we have a commitment proportion of 20%.

With this adjustment in obligation proportion we have a change in Vrms (Root Mean Square estimation of Voltage), when this voltage is given to the ringer it makes an alternate clamor at whatever point there is an adjustment in obligation proportion.

We are gonna to program the UNO to give a PWM sign of various obligation proportion for every one of catches. So we have a tone generator within reach which creates an alternate tone with each catch press.

Components Required

Equipment: Arduino Uno, Power supply (5v), 1000 uF capacitor, 100 nF capacitor, Buzzer, catches (8 pieces).

Programming: AURDINO daily or Atmel studio 6.2

Circuit Diagram as well as Working Explanation

The circuit for tone generator is appeared in underneath outline.

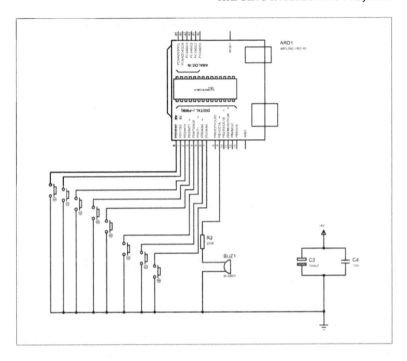

To sift over the clamor from supply voltage capacitors are put crosswise over terminals as appeared in the graph.

The Pulse Width Modulation of Arduino Uno can accomplished at any of pins symbolized as " ~ " on the PCB board. There are 6 Pulse Width Modulation directs in UNO. Anyway we can't utilize PWM pins built up over the PINS 0-7, as the PINS are favored for catches interface.

There is a purpose behind choosing PINS 0-7 as sources of info, on the grounds that the PINS 0-7 speak to the

PORTD of microcontroller. So in the last case we can take the total BYTE of PORTD.

Presently for getting an alternate obligation proportion PWM, we are going to utilize following direction.

analogWrite(9,VALUE);

From above condition we can straightforwardly get the Pulse Width Modulation signal at the comparing pin. The first parameter in quite a while is for picking the stick number of PWM signal. Second parameter is for composing obligation proportion.

The PWM estimation of Arduino Uno can be changed since 0 to 255. With "0" as most minimal to "255" as most elevated. With 255 as obligation proportion we will get 5V at PIN9. In the event that the obligation proportion is given as 125 we will get 2.5V at PIN9. We are going to partition the obligation proportion of 0-250 among 8 catches interfaced at PORTD of UNO. Here I pick 25 increases for each catch, yet it is of your decision.

With that we will have a PWM signal whose obligation proportion changes with each catch. This being given to bell, we have tone generator. Working of this Arduino based tone generator is clarified bit by bit in C code given beneath.

Code

```
void setup()
{
    for (int i=0;i<8;i++)
    {
        pinMode(i, INPUT_PULLUP);//take pins0-7 as
inputs with default high or pulled up pins.
    }
    pinMode(9,OUTPUT);//buzzer output at pin9
}
// the loop routine runs over and over again forever:
void loop()
{
    if(digitalRead(0)==LOW)
    {
        analogWrite(9,25);//if button 1 is pressed
PWM of duty ratio(25*100)/255 is given to buzzer
        delay(100);
        analogWrite(9,0);
    }
    if(digitalRead(1)==LOW)
    {
        analogWrite(9,50); //if button 2 is pressed
PWM of duty ratio(50*100)/255 is given to buzzer
        delay(100);
        analogWrite(9,0);
```

```
      }
   if(digitalRead(2)==LOW)
   {
        analogWrite(9,75);// /if button 3 is pressed
PWM of duty ratio(75*100)/255 is given to buzzer
        delay(100);
        analogWrite(9,0);
   }
   if(digitalRead(3)==LOW)
   {
        analogWrite(9,100); /if button 4 is pressed
PWM of duty ratio(100*100)/255 is given to buzzer
        delay(100);
        analogWrite(9,0);
   }
   if(digitalRead(4)==LOW)
   {
        analogWrite(9,125);
        delay(100);
        analogWrite(9,0);
   }
   if(digitalRead(5)==LOW)
   {
        analogWrite(9,150);
        delay(100);
        analogWrite(9,0);
   }
```

```
    if(digitalRead(6)==LOW)
    {
        analogWrite(9,175);
        delay(100);
        analogWrite(9,0);
    }
    if(digitalRead(7)==LOW)
    {
        analogWrite(9,200);
        delay(100);
        analogWrite(9,0);
    }
}
```

◆ ◆ ◆

7. VARIABLE POWER SUPPLY BY ARDUINO UNO

In this instructional exercise we will build up a 5 V variable voltage source from Arduino Uno. For that we are gonna use Analog to Digital Conversion as well as Pulse Width Modulation highlight.

Some advanced electronic modules like accelerometer deal with voltage 3.3 V as well as some work on 2.2 V. Some even work on lower voltages. With this we can't get a controller for all of them. So here we will make a basic circuit which will give a voltage yield from 0-5 volts at a goals of 0.05V. So with this we may give voltages precisely to different modules.

This circuit can give flows up to 100mA, so we can utilize this power unit for the vast majority of the sensor modules with no issue. This circuit yield can likewise be utilized to charge AA or AAA battery-powered batteries. With the showcase set up we can undoubtedly observe the power changes in the framework. This variable power supply unit contains button interface for the voltage programming. The working as well as circuit is clarified beneath.

Equipment: Arduino Uno, 100uF capacitor (two pieces), button (two pieces), 1K? resistor (three pieces), 16*2 characters LCD, Power supply (5v), 2N2222 transistor.

Programming: Atmel studio 6.2 or AURDINO daily.

Circuit Diagram and Working Explanation

The circuit for variable voltage unit utilizing arduino is appeared in beneath chart.

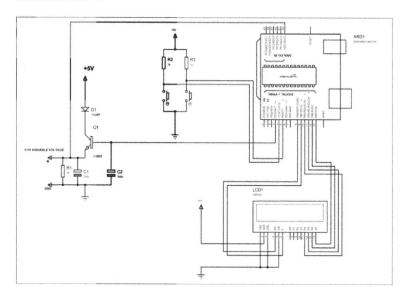

The voltage crosswise over yield isn't totally straight; it will be a loud one. To sift over the commotion capacitors are set crosswise over yield terminals as appeared in figure. The two fastens here are for voltage augmentation and decrement. The presentation unit shows the voltage at the OUTPUT terminals.

Before going for working we have to investigate ADC and PWM highlights of Arduino UNO.

Here we are gonna to take the voltage gave at the OUTPUT terminal as well as feed it into one of ADC channels of Arduino. After change we are going to take that DIGITAL worth and we will relate it to voltage and show the outcome in 16*2 show. This incentive in plain view speaks to the variable voltage esteem.

ARDUINO has six ADC channels, as show in figure. In those any one or every one of them can be utilized as contributions for simple voltage. The UNO ADC is of 10 piece goals (so the number qualities from (0-(2^10) 1023)).This implies that it will guide input voltages somewhere in the range of 0 and 5 volts into whole number qualities somewhere in the range of 0 and 1023. So for each (5/1024= 4.9mV) / unit.

Here we are gonna to utilize A0 of UNO.

1. analogRead(pin);
2. analogReference();
3. analogReadResolution(bits);

Above all else the UNO ADC channels has a default reference estimation of 5V. This implies we can give a most extreme information voltage of 5V for ADC transformation at any information channel. Since certain sensors give voltages from 0-2.5V, with a 5V reference we get lesser precision, so we have a guidance that empowers us to change this reference esteem. So for changing the reference esteem we have ("analogReference();") For now we leave it as.

As default we get the greatest board ADC goals which is 10bits, this goals can be changed by utilizing guidance ("analogReadResolution(bits);"). This goals change can prove to be useful for certain cases. Until further notice we leave it as.

Presently if the above conditions are set to default, the we can peruse an incentive from ADC of channel '0' by legitimately calling capacity "analogRead(pin);", here "stick" speaks to stick where we associated simple sign, for this situation it would be "A0".

The incentive from ADC can be taken into a number as "skim VOLTAGEVALUE = analogRead(A0); ", by this guidance the incentive after ADC gets put away in the whole number "VOLTAGEVALUE".

The PWM of UNO can accomplished at any of pins symbolized as " ~ " on the PCB board. There are six PWM diverts in UNO. We are gonna to utilize PIN3 for our motivation.

analogWrite(3,VALUE);

From above condition we can legitimately get the PWM signal at the relating pin. The first parameter in quite a while is for picking the stick number of PWM signal. Second parameter is for composing obligation proportion.

The PWM estimation of UNO can be changed from 0 to 255. With "0" as most minimal to "255" as most elevated. With 255 as obligation proportion we will get 5V at PIN3. On the off chance that the obligation proportion is given as 125 we will get 2.5V at PIN3

As said before there are two catches associated with PIN4 and PIN5 of UNO. On press the obligation proportion estimation of PWM will increment. At the point when other catch is squeezed the obligation proportion estimation of PWM diminishes. So we are shifting the obligation proportion of PWM signal at PIN3.

This PWM signal at PIN3 is bolstered to the base of NPN transistor. This transistor gives a variable voltage at its producer, while going about as an exchanging gadget.

With the variable obligation proportion PWM at base there will be variable voltage at producer yield. With this we have a variable voltage source close by.

The voltage yield is feed to UNO ADC, for the client to see the voltage yield.

Code

```
#include <LiquidCrystal.h>
LiquidCrystal lcd(8, 9, 10, 11, 12, 13);//
RS,EN,D4,D5,D6,D7
int voltageadjust =125;//starting initial variable output at 2.5V
float check =0;
void setup()
{
     pinMode(3,OUTPUT);//PWM output pin
     pinMode(4,INPUT);//button 1
```

```
        pinMode(5,INPUT);//button 2
        lcd.begin(16, 2);//number of characters on LCD
        // Print a logo message to the LCD.
        lcd.print(" HELLOWORLD");
        lcd.setCursor(0, 1);
        delay (2500);
        delay (2500);
        lcd.clear();
        lcd.print("VOLTAGE= ");//printing name
        lcd.setCursor(9, 0);
}
void loop()
{
        float VOLTAGEVALUE = (analogRead(A0));//read
ADC value at A0
        VOLTAGEVALUE = (VOLTAGEVALUE*5)/1024;//
converting digital value to voltage
        if ((check > (VOLTAGEVALUE+0.05))|(check <
(VOLTAGEVALUE-0.05)))
// if voltage change is higher or lower than 0.5 of previ-
ous value (to avoid fluctuations)
        {
                lcd.print(VOLTAGEVALUE);
                lcd.print("V ");
                lcd.setCursor(9, 0);//go to position 9 on LCD
                check = VOLTAGEVALUE;//store previous
value
```

```
      }
      analogWrite(3,voltageadjust);//provide PWM at
PIN3
      if(digitalRead(4)==LOW)
      {
            if(voltageadjust<250)
            {
                  voltageadjust++;//if button1 is pressed
and value is less than 250 increment the PWM value
                  delay(30);
            }
      }
      if(digitalRead(5)==LOW)
      {
            if(voltageadjust>0)
            {
                  voltageadjust--;// if button2 is pressed
and value is greater than 0 decrement the PWM value
                  delay(30);
            }
      }
      delay(200);
}
```

8. SERVO MOTOR CONTROL BY FLEX SENSOR

In this instructional exercise we will build up a circuit utilizing FLEX sensor, Arduino Uno as well as a Servo engine. This venture is a servo manage framework where the servo shaft position is controlled by the flex or twisted or deviation of the FLEX sensor.

Lets first discussion somewhat about servo engines.

Servo Motors are utilized where there is a requirement for exact shaft development or position. These are not proposed for fast applications. These are proposed for low speed, medium torque as well as precise position application. These engines are utilized in mechanical arm machines, flight controls and control frameworks. Servo engines are utilized in implanted frameworks like candy machines and so forth.

Servo engines are accessible at various shapes and sizes. A servo engine will have basically there wires, one is for positive voltage another is for ground and last one is for position setting. The RED wire is associated with control, Black wire is associated with ground and YELLOW wire is associated with signal.

A servo engine is a mix of DC engine, position control framework, gears. The situation of the pole of the DC engine is balanced by the control hardware in the servo, in light of the obligation proportion of the PWM signal the SIGNAL stick.

Essentially the control gadgets change shaft position by controlling DC engine. This information with respect to position of shaft is sent through the SIGNAL stick. The position information to the control ought to be sent as PWM signal through the Signal stick of servo engine.

The recurrence of PWM (Pulse Width Modulated) sign can fluctuate dependent on sort of servo engine. The significant thing here is the DUTY RATIO of the PWM signal. In view of this DUTY RATION the control hardware alter the pole. For the pole to be moved to 9o clock the TURN ON RATION must be 1/18.ie. one milli second of 'ON schedule' as well as 17 milli second of 'OFF time' in a 18 ms signal.

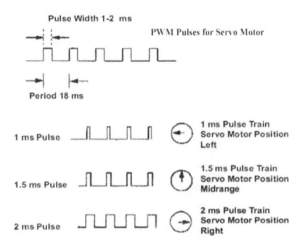

For the pole to be moved to 12o clock the ON time of sign must be 1.5ms and OFF time ought to be 16.5ms. This proportion is decoded by control framework in servo and it modifies the position dependent on it.

This PWM in here is produced by utilizing ARDUINO UNO. So for the time being we realize that, we can control the servo engine shaft by differing the obligation proportion of PWM sign produced by Arduino Uno. The UNO has an uncommon capacity which empowers us to give the situation of SERVO without upsetting the

PWM signal. Anyway it is imperative to know the PWM obligation apportion - servo position connection. We will speak progressively about it in portrayal.

Presently we should discuss FLEX SENSOR. To interface a FLEX sensor to ARDUINO UNO, we are gonna utilize 8 piece Analog to Digital Conversion highlight to carry out the responsibility. A FLEX sensor is a transducer which modifies its obstruction when its shape is changed. A FLEX sensor is of 2.2 inches long or of finger length. It is appeared in figure.

Flex sensor is a transducer which changes its opposition when the straight surface is twisted. Henceforth the name flex sensor. Basically the sensor terminal obstruction increments when it's twisted. This is appeared in beneath figure.

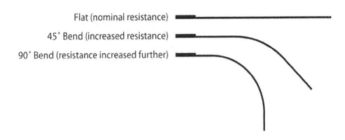

This adjustment in restriction can sit idle worth mentioning except if we can understand them. The current controller can just peruse the odds in voltage and nothing less, for this we are going to utilize voltage divider circuit, with that we can infer the obstruction change as voltage change.

Voltage divider is a resistive circuit and is appeared in figure. In this resistive system we have one consistent obstruction and other variable opposition. As appeared in figure, R1 here is a steady obstruction and R2 is FLEX sensor which goes about as an opposition.

The midpoint of branch is taken to estimation. With R2 modify, we have modify at Vout. So with this we have a voltage which modifies with weight.

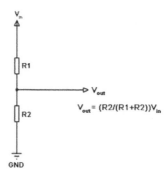

$$V_{out} = (R2/(R1+R2))V_{in}$$

Presently significant thing to note here is, the information taken by the controller for ADC transformation is as low as 50μAmp. This stacking impact of opposition based voltage divider is significant as the current drawn from Vout of voltage divider expands the mistake rate increments, until further notice we need not stress over stacking impact.

FLEX SENSOR when bowed its obstruction changes. With this transducer associated with a voltage divider circuit, we will have a changing voltage with FLEX on transducer. This variable voltage is FED to one of ADC channels, we will have an advanced worth identifying with FLEX.

We will coordinate this computerized an incentive to servo situation, with this we will have servo control by flex.

Components

Equipment: Arduino Uno, 1000 uF capacitor, Power

supply (5v), 100K? resistor, 100nF capacitor (three pieces), 220? resistor, SERVO MOTOR (SG 90), FLEX sensor.

Programming: Atmel studio 6.2 or Aurdino daily.

Circuit Diagram as well as Explanation

The circuit chart for servo engine manage by FLEX sensor is appeared in underneath figure.

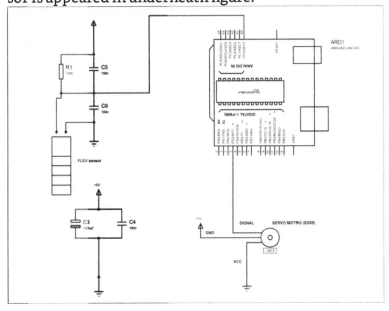

The voltage crosswise over sensor isn't totally direct; it will be an uproarious one. To sift through the clamor, capacitors are put over every resistor in the divider circuit as appeared in figure.

ANBAZHAGAN K

Here we are gonna to take the voltage gave by the divider (voltage which speaks to weight straightly) and feed it into one of ADC Channels of Arduino UNO. We are gonna to utilize A0 for this. After the ADC instatement, we will have computerized worth speaking to the twisted on sensor. We will take this worth and match it with servo position.

For this to happened we have to set up scarcely any directions in program and we will discuss them in detail underneath.

ARDUINO has 6 ADC channels, as show in figure. In those any one or every one of them can be utilized as contributions for simple voltage. The UNO ADC is of 10 piece goals (so the number qualities from (0-(2^10) 1023)).This implies that it will guide input voltages somewhere in the range of 0 and 5 volts into whole number qualities somewhere in the range of 0 and 1023. So for each (5/1024= 4.9mV) / unit.

Here we are gonna to utilize A0 of UNO.

We have to know a couple of things.

1. analogRead(pin);
2. analogReference();
3. analogReadResolution(bits);

As a matter of first importance the UNO ADC channels

has a default reference estimation of 5V. This implies we can give a greatest information voltage of 5V for Analog to Digital Conversion transformation at any info channel. Since certain sensors give voltages from 0-2.5V, with a 5V reference we get lesser exactness, so we have a guidance that empowers us to change this reference esteem. So for changing the reference esteem we have ("analogReference();") For now we leave it as.

As default we get the most extreme board ADC goals which is 10bits, this goals can be changed by utilizing guidance ("analogReadResolution(bits);"). This goals change can prove to be useful for certain cases. Until further notice we leave it as.

Presently if the above conditions are set to default, the we can peruse an incentive from ADC of channel '0' by legitimately calling capacity "analogRead(pin);", here "stick" speaks to stick where we associated simple sign, for this situation it would be "A0".

The incentive from ADC can be taken into a whole number as "int SENSORVALUE = analogRead(A0); ", by this guidance the incentive after ADC gets put away in the number "SENSORVALUE".

Presently how about we talk about the SERVO, the UNO has a component which empowers us to control the servo situation by simply giving the degree esteem. State on the off chance that we need the servo to be at 30, we can legitimately speak to the incentive in the program. The SERVO header document deals with all the obligation proportion computations inside.

```
#include <Servo.h>
Servo servo;
servo.attach(3);
servo.write(degrees);
```

First proclamation speaks to the header document for controlling the SERVO MOTOR.

Second proclamation is naming the servo; we leave it as servo itself.

Third articulation states where the servo sign stick is associated; this must be a PWM stick. Here we are utilizing PIN3.

Fourth articulation gives directions for situating servo engine and is in degrees. In the event that it is given 30, the servo engine pivots 30 degrees.

Presently the sg90 can move from 0-180 degrees, we have ADC result 0-1024

So ADC is around multiple times the SERVO POSITION. So by isolated the ADC result by 6 we will get the rough SERVO hand position.

With this we will have servo position worth bolstered to servo engine, which is in relation to flex or bowed. At the point when this flex sensor mounted on glove, we can manage servo situation by development of hand.

Code

```
#include <Servo.h>
// header for controller servo
Servo servo; //keeping name of servo SERVO itself
int sensorvalue =0;
void setup()
{
    pinMode(A0,INPUT);// voltage divider value input
    pinMode(3,OUTPUT);// PWM output to servo
    servo.attach(3);// telling where signal pin of servo
attached(must be a PWM pin)
}
void loop()
{
    sensorvalue = analogRead(A0); //read analog value
from sensor
        servo.write((sensorvalue-250)/2); //to avoid
initial positioning of servo we need to neutralize the
default voltage provided by voltage divider( setting
servo position based on ADC result)
}
```

◆ ◆ ◆

9. RGB LED WITH ARDUINO

In this undertaking we are gonna to interface five Red Green Blue LEDs to Arduino Uno. These LEDs are associated in parallel for decreasing PIN use of Uno.

A run of the mill RGB LED is appeared in underneath figure:

The RGB LED will have four sticks as appeared in figure.

PIN1: Color 1 negative terminal or shading 1 positive terminal

PIN2: Common positive for every one of the three hues or normal negative for each of the three hues

PIN3: Color 2 negative terminal or shading 2 positive terminal

PIN4: Color 3 negative terminal or shading 3 positive terminal

So there are two kinds of RGB LEDs, one is normal

ANBAZHAGAN K

cathode type (basic negative) and other is basic anode type (regular positive) type. In CC (Common Cathode or Common Negative), there will be three positive terminals every terminal speaking to a shading and one negative terminal speaking to each of the three hues. The inside circuit of a CC RGB LED can be spoken to as underneath.

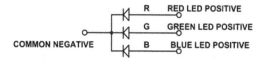

In the event that we need RED to be on in above, we have to control the RED LED stick and ground the normal negative. The equivalent goes for every one of the LEDs. In CA (Common Anode or Common Positive), there will be three negative terminals every terminal speaking to a shading and one positive terminal speaking to each of the three hues. The inner circuit of a CA RGB LED can be spoken to as appeared in figure..

In the event that we need RED to be on in above, we have to ground the RED LED stick and power the normal positive. The equivalent goes for every one of the LEDs.

In our circuit we are gonna to utilize CA (Common Anode or Common Positive) type. For interfacing 5 Red Green Blue LEDs to Arduino we require 5x4= 20 PINS for the most part, by we will decrease this PIN use to 8 by associating Red Green Blue LEDs in parallel as well as by utilizing a system called multiplexing.

Components

Equipment: UNO, 1K? resistor (three pieces), control supply (5v), (Red Green Blue) LED (five pieces)

Programming: Atmel studio 6.2 or Aurdino daily.

Circuit as well as Working Explanation

The circuit association for RGB LED Arduino interfacing is appeared in beneath figure.

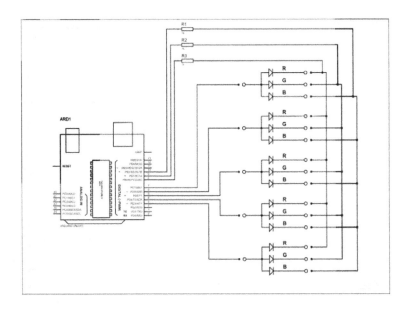

Presently for the precarious part, say we need to turn the RED drove in SET1 as well as GREEN LED in SET2.

We control the PIN8 as well as PIN9 of UNO, as well as ground PIN7, PIN6.

With that stream we will have RED in first SET and GREEN in second SET ON, however we will have GREEN in SET 1 as well as RED in SET2 ON with it. By straightforward relationship we can seen every one of the four LEDs close the circuit with above arrangement thus they all sparkle.

So to wipe out this issue we will turn just each SET on in turn. State at t=0m SEC, SET 1 is tuned ON. At t = 1m SEC, SET 1 is tuned OFF and SET2 is turned ON. Again at t=6m SEC, SET 5 is killed and SET 1 is turned ON. This goes on.

Here the stunt is, the human eye can't catch a recurrence in excess of 30 HZ. That is if a LED goes ON and OFF constantly at a pace of 30HZ or more. The eye considers the To be as constantly ON. Anyway this isn't the situation. The LED will be always turning ON and OFF. This strategy is called multiplexing.

Just talking we self control every basic cathode of 5 SETs 1 milli second, so in 5 milli second we will have finished the cycle, after that the cycle begins from SET 1 once more, this goes on until the end of time. Since the LED SETs are going ON and OFF excessively quick. The human predicts every one of the SETs are ON constantly.

So when we control SET1 at t=0 milli second, we

ground the RED stick. At t=one milli second, we control the SET2 as well as ground the GREEN stick (as of now RED as well as BLUE are pulled up HIGH). The circle goes quick and the eye sees RED sparkle in FIRST SET and GREEN gleam in SECOND SET.

This is the means by which we program a RGB LED, we will sparkle every one of the hues gradually in program to perceive how multiplexing functions.

Code

```
void setup()
{
        for (int i=0;i<11;i++)//all first 11 pins are set as
OUTPUT
        {
            pinMode(i, OUTPUT);
        }
        for (int i=3;i<8;i++)
        {
            digitalWrite(i, LOW);//pins3-8 are set low
        }
}
// the loop routine runs over and over again forever:
void loop()
{
        for (int i=3;i<8;i++)
        {
```

```
        digitalWrite(i,HIGH);//power each set one
time
        for (int j=8;j<11;j++)
        {
            digitalWrite(j,LOW);
            delay(100);
            digitalWrite(j,HIGH);//blink three
colors of each set
        }
        digitalWrite(i,LOW);//pull down power set
after blinking the colors.
    }
}
```

❖ ❖ ❖

10. 8X8 LED MATRIX UTILIZING ARDUINO

In this venture we are going to structure a 8x8 LED lattice show, for that we are going to interface a 8x8 LED grid module with Arduino Uno. A 8x8 LED grid contains 64 LEDs (Light Emitting Diodes) which are orchestrated as a lattice, henceforth the name LED framework.

These networks can be made by circuiting 64 LEDs, anyway that procedure is tedious. Presently a day they are accessible in minimal structures as appeared in underneath picture. These conservative modules are accessible in various sizes as well as numerous hues. The expense of module is same as cost of 64 LEDs, so for specialists this is least demanding to take a shot at.

The uncovered LED framework has 16 stick outs with 8 normal positive and another 8 regular negative. For associating this grid legitimately to an UNO, we have to save 16 sticks on the UNO. With the yield sticks low on UNO, we can't extra 16 PINS. So we have to interface this lattice to a driver chip. This driver chip alongside lattice comes as a set which is appeared in beneath figure.

This module will be interfaced with Arduino for showing letters in order, henceforth the grid show. As a matter of first importance for interfacing LED framework with Arduino, we have to download a library explicitly intended for LED MATRIX. This library will be accessible at: https://github.com/shaai/

Arduino_LED_matrix_sketch/chronicle/master.zip

Subsequent to downloading the Zip record, remove the substance to ARDUINO organizer. (Go to nearby plate where ARDUINO NIGHTLY programming is introduced, open the envelope, scan for organizer named "library", separate the substance of compress record in that envelope, restart the program you will presently have the option to utilize highlights for grid interface)

Components Required

Equipment: Arduino Uno, Power supply (5v), 100 uF capacitor (associated crosswise over power supply)

Programming: Arduino Nightly

Circuit Diagram and Explanation

The associations which are done between Arduino Uno and LED framework module is appeared in beneath table.

PIN2 - - LOAD or CHIPSELECT of LED module

PIN3 - - CLOCK of LED module

PIN4 - - DATAIN of LED module

+5V - - VCC of LED module

GND - - GND of LED module

The circuit outline of 8*8 LED lattice show is appeared in beneath figure.

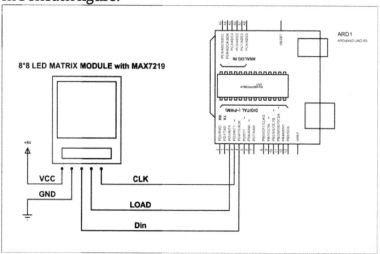

Presently for utilizing the exceptional prospects called by putting in new library, we have to build up not many directions in program and are expressed underneath.

```
#include "LedControlMS.h"
#define NBR_MTX 1
LedControl lc = LedControl(4,3,2, NBR_MTX);
lc.writeString(0,"HELLOWORLD");
lc.clearAll();
```

Initially we have to call the header record for interfacing a LED framework to Arduino Uno. That is" #include "LedControlMS.h"", this header document call the library uncommon capacities.

We have an element with these modules we can associate many number of modules in arrangement and program them all together show. This component proves to be useful when we need a presentation unit which could show numerous characters one after another. So we have to tell the controller what number of showcases we are interfacing.

In this module there are predominantly three pins; information stream from UNO to module takes places with these three pins. The pins are DATAIN (information accepting pin), (clock stick), and CHIPSELECT (direction getting pin).

Presently we have to tell the UNO where we are associating these pins. This is finished by direction "LedControl lc=LedControl(4,3,2, NBR_MTX); ". "lc. writeString(0,"HELLOWORLD");", this order is utilized for disclosing to UNO which characters are to be shown on the LED grid. With the over the showcase appears" HELLOWORLD ", with each character once.

We have to clear the showcase chip memory before sending some other information, this is finished by direction "lc.clearAll();".

By along these lines we can without much of a stretch interface a 8x8 LED grid to Arduino Uno.

Code

```
#include "LedControlMS.h"
//pin 4 is connected to the DataIn
// pin 3 is connected to the CLK
//pin 2 is connected to LOAD
#define NBR_MTX 1 //number of matrices attached is one
LedControl lc=LedControl(4,3,2, NBR_MTX);//
void setup()
{
 for (int i=0; i< NBR_MTX; i++)
 {
  lc.shutdown(i,false);
 /* Set the brightness to a medium values */
  lc.setIntensity(i,8);
 /* and clear the display */
  lc.clearDisplay(i);
      delay(100);
 }
}
void loop()
{
        lc.writeString(0," HELLOWORLD ");//sending characters to display
      lc.clearAll();//clearing the display
      delay(1000);
```

```
}
```

THANK YOU !!!